ANCIENT GREECE

THE HISTORY DETECTIVE INVESTIGATES

Rachel Minay

WAYLAND

First published in 2014 by Wayland

Copyright © Wayland 2014

Wayland
338 Euston Road
London NW1 3BH

Wayland Australia
Level 17/207 Kent Street
Sydney, NSW 2000

The History Detective Investigates series:

Produced for Wayland by
White-Thomson Publishing Ltd
www.wtpub.co.uk
+44 (0)843 208 7460

Editor: Rachel Minay
Designer: Ian Winton
Cover design concept: Lisa Peacock
Consultant: Philip Parker
Proofreader: Lucy Ross

A catalogue record for this title is available from the British Library.

ISBN: 978-0-7502-8180-5
eBook ISBN: 978-0-7502-8549-0

Dewey Number: 938-dc23

Printed in Malaysia

10 9 8 7 6 5 4 3 2 1

Wayland is a division of Hachette Children's Books,
an Hachette UK company

Picture Acknowledgments: Stefan Chabluk:
4; **Corbis:** 27b (Chris Trotman/PCN), **Dreamstime:**
16 (Elizabeth Coughlan), 17b (Panagiotis Karapanagiotis),
24 (George Bailey), 25t (Elena Duvernay); **Shutterstock:**
cover b&t (Nick Pavlakis), folios (ivan bastien), 1 (S.Borisov),
5b (Nick Pavlakis), 6 (Gurgen Bakhshetsyan), 7l (Anastasios71),
8b (Lambros Kazan), 8t (littlewormy), 9t (Kamira), 10
(Anastasios71), 11b (Vladimir Korostyshevskiy), 11t (12_Tribes),
12t (leoks), 14t (Subbotina Anna), 18 (Anastasios71), 20 (Carmen
Ruiz), 21b (Lefteris Papaulakis), 22 (Georgios Kollidas), 23b
(Portokalis), 23t (Anastasios71), 25b (Brigida Soriano), 27t
(Shaiith), 28 (Panos Karas), 29b (Lefteris Papaulakis), 29t (Ralf
Hirsch); **SuperStock:** 21t (ClassicStock.com); **TopFoto:**
7r (CM Dixon/HIP), 13 (AAAC); **Werner
Forman Archive:** 5t (N.J. Saunders), 12b
(British Museum, London); **Wikimedia:**
2 (Marie-Lan Nguyen), 9b (Tilemahos
Efthimiadis), 15b (Jastrow), 15t (Walters
Art Museum), 16 (sailko), 17t (Walters
Art Museum), 19b (cgGJhGb6MjVeAw
at Google Cultural Institute), 19t
(Marie-Lan Nguyen), 26 (Tedmek).

Above: There are many pictures of the Minotaur in ancient art. According to Greek legend, the terrifying half-bull, half-man lived at the centre of a maze on the island of Crete.

Previous page: This ruined temple at Cape Sounion, Greece, was dedicated to Poseidon, god of the sea. The captain of a ship often made an offering to Poseidon before sailing, in the hope of a safe journey.

Cover (top): The Parthenon.

Cover (bottom): The 'Mask of Agamemnon' (see page 5).

CONTENTS

Words in **bold** can be found in the glossary on page 30.

 The history detective Sherlock Bones will help you to find clues and collect evidence about ancient Greece. Wherever you see one of Sherlock's paw-prints, you will find a mystery to solve. The answers are on page 31.

WHO WERE THE ANCIENT GREEKS?

Greece is a mountainous country in southern Europe with a warm and sunny climate. It is made up of mainland Greece and many islands, and is almost surrounded by the sea. In ancient times it was known as Hellas and was home to one of the greatest civilizations in world history.

The ancient Greeks were people who lived in this area more than 2,000 years ago. Ancient Greece is sometimes called the 'birthplace' or the 'cradle' of western civilization because the ancient Greeks led the way in so many areas of life – for example in art, architecture, politics and science.

The Odyssey is a famous ancient Greek poem that tells the story of Odysseus, a hero who battles gods and monsters. It is thought to have been written by a poet called Homer. This is how Crete is described in *The Odyssey*:

'Out in the middle of the wine-dark sea, there is a land called Crete, a rich and lovely land washed by the sea on every side; and in it are many peoples and 90 cities. ... Among the cities is Knossos, a great city; and there Minos was nine years king...'

This map shows the main sites in ancient Greece and the surrounding area.

The **Minoans** were the first great civilization in this part of the world. Based on the large island of Crete, their culture developed from about 3200 BCE. The Minoans became rich through trade and built elaborate palaces decorated with beautiful **frescoes**. An **archaeologist** called Arthur Evans **excavated** a palace at Knossos in 1900. He gave the civilization the name 'Minoan' after the legendary ruler of Crete, King Minos.

👣 **How did the Minoan civilization get its name?**

The **Mycenaeans** lived on mainland Greece around the city of Mycenae from about 1600 to 1100 BCE. Some historians consider them to be the first Greeks: they spoke a form of the Greek language and wrote using a system of symbols that we call **Linear B**. They were a warlike and powerful people. According to the legend of the Trojan War (see page 24), Agamemnon, the king of Mycenae, led the Greeks to fight against the city of Troy, now in Turkey.

The Mycenaean civilization ended around 1100 BCE, probably as a result of invasion. Historians know very little about the 'dark ages' that followed, but from about 500 BCE Greece entered what is sometimes called a golden age. This is a period of time when people make great cultural improvements, such as incredible buildings or works of art. In ancient Greece, this is known as the **Classical** period, and it was a time when art, architecture, literature, science and **philosophy** flourished.

This Minoan fresco shows two women standing either side of a bull while a man leaps acrobatically over its back. Bull-leaping may have been part of a religious ceremony.

DETECTIVE WORK

Why did the Minoan civilization end? Nobody knows exactly! Explore one theory at: http://www.bbc.co.uk/history/ancient/greeks/minoan_01.shtml

This gold mask was found by an archaeologist called Heinrich Schliemann in a grave at Mycenae in 1876. Schliemann claimed it was the funeral mask of Agamemnon, but modern archaeology suggests it was from a much earlier period. Some even believe that Schliemann added the moustache himself!

WHAT WAS A CITY-STATE?

Ancient Greece was not one single country but a collection of states that were based around a city or an island. Each *polis*, or city-state, was independent from the others, but they shared the same beliefs and the same language.

The mountainous country made farming difficult, so most Greek city-states developed around the coast. The sea was very important to the city-states – both as a source of food and for transport for trading or war. The Greeks also set up **colonies** in other parts of Europe, Asia and North Africa.

A city-state was made up of a city and the surrounding countryside. The major city-states were Athens, Sparta, Thebes, Corinth and Argos and they had their own systems of government and their own customs. The city-states often went to war with one another but sometimes joined together to fight a common enemy. Athens (see pages 8–9) was the largest and most powerful city, but at times in its history Sparta rivalled Athens.

(see pages 8–9)

DETECTIVE WORK

Find out more by visiting the city-states of Athens and Sparta: http://www.hyperstaffs. info/work/history/miller/ ancientgreece.swf

These ruins were once part of a temple in the city-state of Corinth. Corinth was a centre of trade and pottery-making.

Sparta was a city-state of brave warriors and Spartans considered strength and the ability to fight to be more important than anything else. Life in Sparta was extremely tough. Babies were examined by an official group of elders and those who were considered too weak were left to die. At the age of seven, boys had to leave their families and live in **barracks** with the other soldiers to learn how to fight and wrestle. Girls and women were expected to be fit and strong so they would give birth to healthy Spartan babies.

Women and girls in Sparta had more freedom than in other parts of ancient Greece. Spartan girls – like the one depicted in this bronze statue – were also taught to race and wrestle.

Ancient Greek city-states usually followed the same design. The most important government buildings and temples formed part of the **acropolis**, which was always placed at the highest point of the city. There was also an **agora**, which was the marketplace and main meeting area, and a theatre (see pages 18–19). City walls helped to protect the city from attack and the countryside outside the city walls was used for farming.

The word 'acropolis' means 'high city' and the people who designed Greek cities always put the acropolis at the highest point. Why do you think that was?

Acropolis

The ancient acropolis can still be seen high above the modern city of Athens.

WHY WAS ATHENS IMPORTANT?

By the middle of the fifth century BCE, Athens was the largest, richest and most powerful city-state in Greece. Hundreds of thousands of people lived in the city and in the surrounding region, which was called Attica. The patron goddess of the city was Athena, goddess of wisdom, and Athens prided itself on being a great centre for learning and the arts.

Athens became wealthy because it was near the sea, which was essential for trade, and because it could source silver and marble from the local area. It used the marble to construct some of the most incredible buildings in ancient Greece. Like other Greek cities, Athens had an acropolis, which contained a group of beautiful temples, an agora and a theatre. The most impressive building on the acropolis was the Parthenon, a temple to the goddess Athena.

🐾 The caryatid sculptures are beautiful to look at, but they have another purpose. What is it?

These sculptures, called caryatids, form part of another temple on the acropolis.

The Parthenon was carved from marble and decorated with the finest sculptures. This classical style of architecture has been copied all over the world.

Parthenon

DETECTIVE WORK
Discover more about Athens' Acropolis at the British Museum and design your own temple: http://www.ancientgreece.co.uk/acropolis/home_set.html

In Classical times, Athens would have been a bustling, lively city. Many people lived and worked here while others came to study or to trade. The agora would have been full of people buying and selling food, wine, slaves and horses. Men would also meet friends here to talk business or politics.

Our word 'politics' comes from the Greek word for 'city-state' – *polis*. The various city-states had different forms of government. Some, like Corinth, were **monarchies** (ruled by kings). Some, like Sparta, were **oligarchies** (ruled by a small group of people). Athens invented a new form of government called **democracy** – or government by the people. In this system, the rules were made by the citizens, whether they were rich or poor. However, citizens meant men who had been born in the city and whose parents had been born there too – women, slaves and people from other cities were not allowed to be citizens.

A great and wealthy city has to protect itself from invasion, and Athens did this with the help of a fearsome navy. Because Greece has a long coastline, ruling the seas was necessary in order to survive, and after 490 BCE Athens built hundreds of warships called **triremes** to defend its wealth and position. Ships that were used for trade were usually powered by sails alone, but triremes combined sails and many oars to move quickly through the water and attack enemy ships.

Pericles was a famous Athenian politician and military leader who lived from about 495 to 429 BCE. An impressive speaker, he encouraged the arts and literature and ordered the construction of the Parthenon.

Athenians could vote to send someone unpopular away from the city. They voted on pieces of pottery, called ostraka. These ostraka show the names of Megacles, who was sent away in 486 BCE, and his father Hippocrates.

Pericles supported democracy. This is from a speech he gave, as it was reported by the historian Thucydides:

'Our constitution does not copy the laws of neighbouring states; we are rather a pattern to others than imitators ourselves. Its administration favours the many instead of the few; this is why it is called a democracy.'

WHAT ARE THE GREEK MYTHS?

The ancient Greeks were polytheistic, which means they believed in many gods and goddesses rather than just one. They used these gods to explain the world as they saw it and their belief in the gods affected many aspects of their lives. These beliefs and stories about the gods are called the Greek myths.

The Greeks believed that the most important gods lived at the top of Mount Olympus, Greece's highest mountain, and that pleasing them meant good harvest and good fortune. They built many temples to their gods and gave them presents of food, wine and sometimes a slaughtered animal. They did not believe that they had to live a 'good life' to please the gods, but they lived in fear of being punished for making the gods angry.

Delphi was an important religious site. People came from all over Greece to ask the advice of the 'oracle', a priestess who was said to be able to see the future.

> 'All men have need of the gods.'
>
> Homer, *The Odyssey*

DETECTIVE WORK

Which is your favourite Greek myth? Listen to lots of amazing legends at this site:
http://storynory.com/category/greek-myths/

Zeus	king of the gods
Hera	queen of the gods and goddess of marriage
Hades	god of the underworld
Poseidon	god of the sea
Demeter	goddess of farming
Apollo	god of music, poetry and light
Artemis	goddess of the moon and hunting
Ares	god of war
Hephaestus	god of fire
Hermes	messenger of the gods
Aphrodite	goddess of love and beauty
Dionysus	god of wine and drama
Athena	goddess of wisdom and the patron goddess of Athens

This table shows the main Greek gods and goddesses. All except Hades, who ruled over the kingdom of the dead, were believed to live on Mount Olympus.

The ancient Greeks loved storytelling. They told many stories about the gods who they believed could live forever but who in other ways were quite like humans – for example, they spent a lot of time arguing among themselves! Some of the stories helped the Greeks to explain the mysteries of the natural world, such as the creation of the world, the sun appearing to move across the sky, the seasons and disasters such as earthquakes.

🐾 **Which Greek god is depicted on this jar?**

The Greeks also loved tales about great heroes, including Odysseus, Heracles, Jason and Perseus. These heroes had to battle terrifying monsters, such as Medusa, who had snakes instead of hair and could turn people into stone, a one-eyed giant called the Cyclops, and Cerberus, the three-headed dog who guarded the gates of the underworld.

Heracles (who the Romans called Hercules) was a legendary Greek hero. The son of the god Zeus and a human woman, he had superhuman powers and had to undertake twelve 'labours' or tasks – including killing the Hydra, a many-headed monster.

WHAT WAS DAILY LIFE LIKE?

Daily life in ancient Greece depended on the city-state you were from, whether you were rich or poor and whether you were a man, a woman or a child.

Like Greek houses today, those in ancient times were painted white to reflect the hot sun.

Greek homes were built from mud bricks and had tiled roofs. Poor families had smaller homes with one main room for eating, shared bedrooms and simple furniture. Richer families had bigger homes built around a central courtyard. Furniture was more decorative than in poorer homes and there were colourful tapestries on the walls. There were separate rooms in a wealthy home for men, women and slaves.

The women and girls from rich families had almost no freedom and were expected to stay at home, often in the women's room. Poorer women had more freedom as they could visit the agora to buy food or meet friends. Both boys and girls were expected to give up their toys aged twelve to show they had grown up, and many girls were married at about fifteen. Some Greek girls had a little education at home, but boys from rich families went to school at the age of seven to be taught reading, writing, arithmetic, music and sports.

DETECTIVE WORK

Our word 'alphabet' comes from the first two letters in the Greek alphabet, *alpha* and *beta*. Find out more about Greek writing here: http://www.childrensuniversity.manchester.ac.uk/interactives/history/greece/alphabet/

These women are playing the popular game of knucklebones, in which five small bones were thrown and caught on the hand. The modern version is often called jacks.

Rich men worked in politics or as **merchants**, so rich people tended to live in towns where it was easy for men to go to work and visit the agora. Rich people also had slaves to do the hard work in their homes or on their farms. Some families might have as many as fifty slaves. However, most people in ancient Greece were poor. They lived in villages and earned a basic living by farming enough food to keep their own family, possibly having enough to trade for other goods at the agora.

Slaves worked as miners (as in this picture), servants, cooks, nurses and labourers.

Rich people often rode horses, while the poor had to walk, but the mountainous country made travel difficult for everyone and going on a journey was a risky business. Travellers might face robbers on the path or have to go a very long way round if city-states were at war. It was often quicker to travel by ship, but some sailors robbed their passengers and there was always a danger of pirates!

Beautiful plates like this would have been used in the homes of rich people. This plate from about 530 BCE shows a story from the Greek myths about the god Dionysus being attacked by pirates.

In the story, Dionysus turned the pirates into animals as they leapt into the sea. What animals?

WHAT DID THE ANCIENT GREEKS EAT AND DRINK?

How does your diet compare to that of an ancient Greek? Their breakfast was usually bread soaked in wine or olive oil. Lunch might have been bread with cheese, olives and figs. The evening meal might have been porridge with vegetables, perhaps with fish, cheese or eggs.

Most of the country was too mountainous for farming, but the higher slopes on hills were used to grow olives. Wine was a common drink for all Greeks and the grapes to make it were grown on the lower slopes. In the few places where the ground was **fertile**, farmers grew barley, which was made into bread and porridge, and sometimes wheat. Because there was so little rain during the summer, grain crops were sown in October to grow through the winter and spring. Farmers also grew fruit and vegetables, which townspeople could buy in the agora.

All Greeks ate fish and seafood, which were abundant in the waters around the coast. Meat was not widely eaten, especially by the poor, but the rich would sometimes hunt birds, hares, deer and wild boar for meat.

The Mediterranean climate is ideal for growing olive trees. Then, as now, olives were grown to eat and to make olive oil. In Athens, it was a crime to pull up an olive tree.

Philosophers are people who speak about life and how humans behave. The philosopher Socrates had a warning for his fellow ancient Greeks about eating and drinking habits:

'Bad men live that they may eat and drink, whereas good men eat and drink that they may live.'

This beautiful fresco from Knossos shows a sea that is full of fish and dolphins. Both rich and poor Greeks ate fish, as well as seafood such as octopus and squid.

Ancient Greek pottery was often beautifully made and decorated. It was usually one of two types – a red pot decorated with black figures or a black pot decorated with red figures. One of the reasons that we know so much about the ancient Greeks is because a lot of the pottery has survived and because it is often decorated with pictures of everyday life.

The rich in ancient Greece ate very well at times of feasting and celebration. A feast menu might include roast pig stuffed with thrushes, oysters and cake, all washed down with a lot of wine. A **symposium** was a popular drinking party, which was held by the man of the house for male friends. On arrival, the guests had their hands and feet washed by slaves. Then they ate food, drank wine and discussed topics such as love or politics.

Guests at a symposium lay on couches rather than sat up. They were often entertained by hired acrobats or musicians.

This wine cup from about 480 BCE is an example of red-figure pottery.

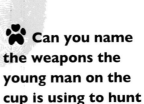

Can you name the weapons the young man on the cup is using to hunt the boar?

DETECTIVE WORK

Greek pots are often decorated with repeating patterns and pictures that tell a story. Copy some typical patterns and decorate a vase by printing out the activity at: http://www.schoolsliaison. org.uk/kids/siteactivities/ greekvase.pdf

HOW DID THE ANCIENT GREEKS DRESS?

Surviving objects and paintings tell us a lot about ancient Greek clothes, hairstyles and jewellery. The Greeks also cared about beauty and hygiene, washing regularly, rubbing olive oil into the skin and wearing perfume and make-up.

Fabrics were made from sheep's wool or a plant called flax, which was used to make linen. They were woven on looms in the home and then made into simple tunics, which were often belted and pinned in place and then hung down in folds. Clothes could be white or brightly coloured with the use of plant and animal dyes.

DETECTIVE WORK

Find out more about ancient Greek dress at the Metropolitan Museum of Art: http://www. metmuseum.org/toah/hd/ grdr/hd_grdr.htm

This gravestone, which dates from about 100 BCE, shows a Greek woman with a child who is probably her slave. The woman is wearing a classic sleeveless belted tunic, with bracelets on her wrists and upper arms.

The two most popular forms of tunic were called the *peplos* – a sleeveless tunic that was pinned at the shoulders and gathered and folded at the waist – and the *chiton*, a looser tunic that was often sewn and sometimes had sleeves. Just like today, fashions changed over time. In the early period of ancient Greece, the fashion was for highly patterned, bright tunics that were quite close-fitting. Later fashions were for plainer fabrics in looser designs. By the fourth century BCE, Greek style had changed again to the patterned fabrics and closer-fitting style of the early period.

The clothes worn by ancient Greeks were made of fabrics that have not survived to the present day. How do you think historians know what they wore?

Both rich and poor liked to wear jewellery such as earrings, necklaces and rings. The poor might wear jewellery made from bronze or pottery; the rich could afford gold, silver, ivory and precious stones. As people were often buried with their jewellery, many pieces have been found in tombs by archaeologists.

Jewellery made from precious metals such as gold or silver showed how rich a person was.

Footwear meant simple leather sandals or boots, although it was common for Greeks to go barefoot. It was usual to wear a hat with a brim to keep the hot sun off in summer. Both men and women might also wear a *himation* – a wrap or cloak that was thin and light for summer or thick and warm in winter.

This Minoan wall painting shows women's hairstyles in detail. As with fashion, hairstyles changed over time. Greek women usually wore their hair long, but during some periods it was tied up with decorative pins, bands or ribbons.

WHAT HAPPENED AT A GREEK THEATRE?

The ancient Greeks loved drama, music and poetry and a theatre was an important part of many Greek cities. Theatres were built in the open air and could hold thousands of people.

The idea of performing plays in a theatre began as a religious festival in honour of the god Dionysus. In Athens, this festival became an annual event that included processions, sacrifices and drama competitions where playwrights entered to win prizes. Watching plays became so popular that people started to build enormous theatres all over Greece.

A Greek theatre was built in a semicircular shape and the **tiered** stone seating meant that the audience could all see and hear the actors below. Actors were always men. A group of performers, called the **chorus**, commented on the action of the play by singing or dancing together in the semicircular area known as the **orchestra**. The actors appeared on a stage in front of a building called a **skene**. It was sometimes painted to look like a background for the play, and is where we get the word 'scenery' from.

How does this ancient theatre look similar to a modern one?

This ancient theatre is in Delphi.

Plays were either comedies or tragedies. Comedies were funny plays that included rude jokes and **slapstick** and were often about ordinary people. Tragedies were often about gods and heroes and the main character usually came to a horrible end! Well-known Greek playwrights include Aeschylus, Sophocles, Euripides and Aristophanes. Their plays are still performed today.

As well as drama, the ancient Greeks enjoyed music, dancing and poetry. The most famous Greek poet was Homer, who is thought to have written the epic poems *The Iliad* and the *The Odyssey*. Lyric poetry was another kind of poetry, where the words were accompanied by the music of a lyre.

DETECTIVE WORK

Discover more about Greek theatre and visit one via the 'Activities' link at: http://www.bbc.co.uk/schools/primaryhistory/ancient_greeks/arts_and_theatre/

Actors wore masks, like this one of the god Dionysus. The expression on the mask often told the audience something about the character. The large features meant that the expression could be seen even at the back of the theatre.

This nineteenth-century painting shows the lyric poet Sappho listening to another poet, Alcaeus. The artist wanted the painting to be as realistic as possible, so he copied the seating from the theatre of Dionysus in Athens.

WHEN WERE THE FIRST OLYMPIC GAMES?

The modern Olympic Games are the world's biggest sporting event. The Summer Olympics and the Winter Olympics are each held every four years and it is every athlete's dream to participate in the Olympics and represent their country. The modern event first took place in 1896, but the origins of the Olympic Games lie much further back in history – in ancient Greece.

Discus throwing was part of the pentathlon event, which also included javelin, running, long jump and wrestling.

The first Olympics are believed to have taken place in 776 BCE and were held at Olympia in honour of Zeus, the king of the gods. Like the modern Olympics, they took place every four years. Sprinting was the only sport at the first Olympics, but other sports were added over time and the Games became a major five-day event. There were fast and furious chariot races with as many as forty chariots taking part at once, boxing matches that only ended when one boxer gave up or passed out, and violent wrestling events.

What did athletes wear in ancient Greece?

DETECTIVE WORK

Learn more and follow the link to visit the ancient Olympic Games: http://www.bbc.co.uk/schools/ primaryhistory/ancient_greeks/ the_olympic_games/

A modern city that hosts the Olympics has special buildings to house the different events and impress the visitors to the Games – and ancient Olympia did this, too. It must have been an amazing moment for the athletes and other visitors when they entered the Temple of Zeus. It contained an enormous statue of the god made from gold and ivory. The athletes had to take an oath and make sacrifices to Zeus before the Games began.

Only men could compete in the Games. Unmarried women were allowed to watch, but married women were not allowed to attend at all. This was because they were considered the property of their husbands, who rarely allowed them to meet or talk to other men and it was not considered suitable for them to see the naked athletes.

The Olympic Games were so important that city-states were not allowed to go to war with each other while they took place. Men travelled from all over Greece and beyond to compete and victory was a matter of pride for individual city-states. Winners were crowned with olive leaves and returned to their home cities in glory.

The statue of Zeus at Olympia was so incredible that people considered it one of the seven wonders of the ancient world.

A winner at the ancient Games was presented with a crown of olive leaves rather than a medal. This twentieth-century stamp shows ancient Greeks cutting a branch from an olive tree to make a victory crown.

Pausanias was a second-century Greek who travelled through the country recording what he saw. He was very impressed by the Games, as well as by secret religious ceremonies known as the Eleusinian rites:

'Many are the sights to be seen in Greece, and many are the wonders to be heard; but on nothing does Heaven bestow more care than on the Eleusinian rites and the Olympic games.'

WHO WERE THE GREEK PHILOSOPHERS?

Some ancient Greeks were great thinkers. They liked debating, or discussing, ideas about life, knowledge and their society. These ancient Greeks were known as philosophers, and their ideas continue to have meaning to this day.

The word 'philosophy' means 'love of wisdom' and philosophy is the study of knowledge, truth and human existence. The three most famous ancient Greek philosophers were Socrates, Plato and Aristotle.

Socrates was born in Athens and lived from about 469 to 399 BCE. He was known for using a series of questions to help someone examine their own knowledge and beliefs – this is now called the 'Socratic method'. Socrates did not write down his own ideas; the reason we know so much about him was because another philosopher, Plato, did write down what Socrates had taught.

Socrates' radical ideas were not popular with many people in Athens. Eventually he was tried for not respecting the gods and corrupting young people. He was sentenced to death by drinking poison.

What does the word 'philosophy' mean?

Plato lived from about 427 to 347 BCE. He was influenced by Socrates but also had his own philosophical ideas. It was Plato who wrote about the mythical island of Atlantis, which he said existed 9,000 years before and which in 'one grievous day and night… was swallowed up by the sea and vanished'. One of the things Plato was interested in was what made an ideal society and he may have used the story of Atlantis to explain his ideas. However, the mythical island of Atlantis – and whether it was fact or fiction – has fascinated and intrigued people for centuries.

Aristotle lived from 384 to 322 BCE. He was not just a philosopher but one of the first great scientists. He studied many different subjects including poetry, zoology, politics and psychology. As well as teaching at Plato's Academy, Aristotle also founded his own place of study, the Lyceum.

▶ **In about 387 BCE, Plato founded the Academy in Athens. This was like a very early university and Aristotle was a pupil and a teacher there.**

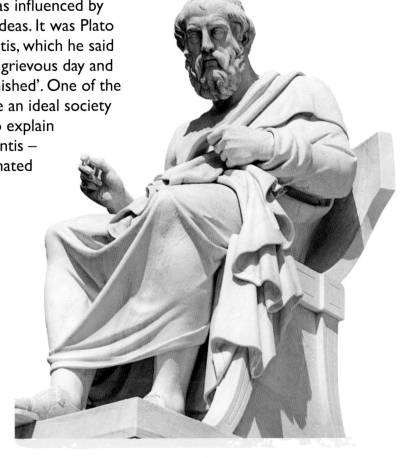

DETECTIVE WORK

Find out more about Socrates, Plato and Aristotle at: http://library.thinkquest.org/CR0210200/ancient_greece/philosophers.htm

Aristotle was one of the teachers of the powerful Macedonian king, Alexander the Great (see page 25).

Here are some quotations by the ancient Greek philosophers. Do you agree with them?

'*Friendship is a single soul dwelling in two bodies.*' (Aristotle)

'*He who has overcome his fears will truly be free.*' (Aristotle)

'*A wise man speaks because he has something to say; a fool because he has to say something.*' (Plato)

'*The only true wisdom is in knowing you know nothing.*' (Socrates)

WHY DID THE ANCIENT GREEKS FIGHT WARS?

The ancient Greeks fought many battles and wars. The rival city-states were often quarrelling and fighting with each other. However, they sometimes came together to fight against a common enemy.

The Trojan War is a conflict mentioned in Greek mythology in which Mycenaean warriors attacked the city of Troy in around 1200 BCE. The ancient Greeks who came later, such as Homer in his *Iliad*, told amazing stories about it that included gods and goddesses, heroes and the Trojan horse – a trick that the Greeks played on the Trojans and which led to their defeat. For many years, historians thought the Trojan War was just a legend, but archaeological remains near Hisarlik in Turkey indicate that this may have been the city of Troy. The remains of the city also show signs of destruction for the period the war was supposed to have occurred in.

DETECTIVE WORK

Explore the world of ancient Greek warfare at: http://www.ancientgreece.co.uk/war/home_set.html

Legend tells how the Greeks secretly hid soldiers inside the Trojan horse. At night, the soldiers crept out and opened the city gates to let the rest of the Greek army into Troy.

War was based on land or at sea. On land, the most powerful units were foot soldiers known as **hoplites** who fought in a strong block formation called a **phalanx**. Soldiers in a phalanx were well protected by their wall of shields, but if a soldier at the front was killed, he was replaced by the man behind. At sea, the best warship was the trireme. During the fifth century BCE, the Greeks came together to fight invasions from Persia, a vast empire that stretched from Egypt to India. Major battles included the Battle of Marathon, on land, in 490 BCE and a large naval battle at Salamis in 480 BCE.

The city-states were often at war with each other. The Peloponnesian War, which lasted for twenty-seven years (431–404 BCE), pitted the fearsome land army of Sparta against the mighty navy of Athens. Sparta finally won this war, but the victory did not last long and within the next fifty years, most of Greece was swallowed up by the empire of Alexander the Great.

Alexander the Great was born in the ancient kingdom of Macedonia, in the northeast of Greece, in 356 BCE. He became king at the age of twenty. A remarkable military leader, he conquered the mighty Persian empire and was undefeated in battle. By the time of his death, Alexander's empire stretched from Greece in the west to India in the east and south into Egypt, and he had spread Greek language and culture throughout the region.

Alexander was only thirty-two when he died. After his death, the colossal empire he had built up began to weaken and split. Greece would never be so powerful again.

The trireme was a fast warship, with three rows of oars on each side. It attacked an enemy ship by ramming, making big holes in its side and throwing its sailors into the water on impact.

'Tri' means 'three', so why do you think the trireme got this name?

'There is nothing impossible to him who will try.'

Alexander the Great

WHAT IS THE LEGACY OF ANCIENT GREECE?

Greece eventually became part of the Roman Empire in 146 BCE, but the Romans were impressed and inspired by the Greek world and adopted many aspects of it into their own civilization. This influence has continued throughout European history.

One of the most significant legacies of ancient Greece is that of democracy, the form of government first practised in Athens during the Classical period. It's hard for us to imagine what a new idea this was. Giving the people a say in how their city was run was very different to one person (or a few people) making all the rules and then telling the people what the rules were. Although the ancient Greek form of democracy was not entirely democratic – neither women nor slaves were allowed to vote as citizens – many modern governments are based on the principles of democracy.

The great thinkers of ancient Greece have also left their mark on modern times. The work of mathematicians such as Pythagoras and scientists such as Archimedes are still relevant today. Some ancient astronomers knew that the planets move around the Sun and how to measure the distance of the Sun from the Earth. And although Greek views of medicine were closely tied to religion, they understood the importance of exercise, food and hygiene to good health.

DETECTIVE WORK

Read this article by historian Michael Scott to find out how Greek democracy differs from our own and why our idea of Classical architecture is different from how the Greeks saw it: http://www.historyextra.com/blog/what-did-ancient-greeks-do-us

Hippocrates is known as the 'father of modern medicine'. He believed in examining patients closely, observing their symptoms and treating the body as a whole. He wrote a guide for how doctors should behave. This is called the 'Hippocratic Oath' and it still has meaning for doctors today.

The elegant buildings of ancient Greece were copied both by the Romans and by later architects. The Renaissance, which means 'rebirth', was a period in history from the fourteenth to the seventeenth centuries. During the Renaissance, people looked back at the Classical period to inspire architecture, art, science and philosophy.

Edinburgh's classical-style architecture has led to the city being called the 'Athens of the North'.

As well as the surviving art and architecture, the Greeks also left us poetry, plays and the basic design of our modern theatres. And did you know that the Greeks also gave us many words, such as 'history', 'geography', 'enthusiasm', 'magic', 'organize' and 'technology'? Perhaps this – their gift to the English language – is the greatest legacy of this amazing ancient civilization.

What do you think is the most significant legacy of ancient Greece? Perhaps you think it's the modern Olympics – the world's greatest sporting event. Now, as then, the important thing for athletes was taking part and gaining pride for their homeland.

YOUR PROJECT

By now you will be aware of how much the ancient Greeks have given to the modern world. There are so many aspects of Greek culture that you could choose for your project, but think carefully about what interests you and what you would like to study in depth. What will you choose to research and present from this brilliant civilization?

You could choose any of the topics covered in this book to focus on – for example you could write a detailed study of the Olympic Games, the Minoan or Mycenaean civilizations, the fashion of ancient Greece, or its archaeology (who were the major archaeologists and what did they find?).

Alternatively, you could write a biography of a famous Greek such as Pericles, Alexander the Great, the poet Sappho or Hippocrates. Or you could write an imaginary day-in-the-life story of an ordinary person in ancient Greece – perhaps a girl growing up in Sparta, a slave working in Athens or a young warrior fighting in one of the ancient Greek wars.

Another idea would be to organize a philosophical debate. You could choose a subject that might have interested Socrates, such as 'What is truth?' or 'What is beauty?' or you could choose a topic that relates the ancient Greek world to the modern one, such as 'What is the greatest legacy of ancient Greece?' or 'Is it right that many ancient Greek artefacts are in British museums?' Whichever side of the argument you choose to defend, you will have to do a lot of research to make a good case.

Your project could be centred around one of the Greek myths. You could rewrite and illustrate the story or present it as a play. Perhaps you could even make Greek-style actors' masks or include a chorus to comment on the action!

You could write a biography of Leonidas, the king of Sparta. He fought bravely against huge odds at the Battle of Thermopylae.

Project presentation

● Do plenty of research for your project. Use the Internet and your local or school library.

● If you are writing a diary or a biography of an ancient Greek, imagine what questions you would ask them and what they might answer.

● Collect as many pictures as you can to illustrate your project. Print off images from the Internet or draw items that you see in museums. Will your project need a map or timeline?

● If you are organizing a debate, what questions will you need to ask and answer?

▶ **The beautiful frescoes at Knossos are a glimpse into the life and culture of the Minoans.**

Look in books or online for examples of ancient Greek buildings, such as these ruins at Delphi, and find out what happened inside them.

GLOSSARY

acropolis A fortified part of an ancient Greek city, often built on a hill.

agora An open space in an ancient Greek city, used as a market and a meeting place.

archaeologist Someone who studies the remains of past societies.

barracks A building used to house soldiers.

BCE 'Before the Common Era'. Used to signify years before the believed birth of Jesus, around 2,000 years ago.

chorus A group of actors who speak together to comment on a play.

Classical The period of ancient Greek history from about 500 BCE to 336 BCE.

colony A city founded by settlers from another city and usually under the control of the original city.

corrupt Influence in a bad way.

democracy A form of government in which the people have a say in how the state or country is ruled.

excavate Remove earth from the ground in order to find buried remains.

fertile Able to produce a lot of plants or crops.

fresco A wall painting made quickly on wet plaster.

hoplite A well-armed ancient Greek foot soldier.

Linear B A way of writing Mycenaean Greek. Linear B was deciphered (decoded or understood) in the 1950s.

merchant Someone whose job is trading things.

Minoan An ancient civilization based on Crete, whose culture developed from about 3200 BCE.

monarchy A form of government in which the people are ruled by monarchs (kings or queens).

Mycenaean An ancient civilization that lived on mainland Greece around the city of Mycenae from about 1600 BCE to 1100 BCE.

oligarchy A form of government in which a small group of people are in control.

orchestra The semicircular area in a theatre where the chorus performed.

ostraka Pieces of pottery that Athenians used when voting to send someone away from the city.

patron goddess The guardian or protecting goddess of a certain place.

phalanx A block of soldiers standing or moving in formation.

philosophy The study of knowledge, truth and human existence.

slapstick Comedy to do with clumsiness and embarrassing situations.

skene The building in a theatre where the actors changed and which was used as a background.

symposium A drinking party, often held after a banquet.

tiered With rows or levels placed one above the other.

trireme A fast warship with three rows of oars on each side.

ANSWERS

Page 4:   The archaeologist Arthur Evans gave the Minoans their name because they lived on Crete, which was associated with the legendary king Minos.

Page 7:   The acropolis was always at the highest point so it could be defended against attack.

Page 8:   The caryatid sculptures help to support the building.

Page 11:   The god is playing a musical instrument, so it must be Apollo, the god of music.

Page 13:   Dionysus has turned the pirates into dolphins.

Page 15:   He is using two spears. He also has a short sword tied to his waist.

Page 16:   From pictures on surviving pottery, sculptures such as the gravestone shown, and other art. We also know from descriptions written by people who lived at the time.

Page 18:   There is tiered seating around a central area so that all spectators can have a view of the performance.

Page 20:   Athletes wore nothing.

Page 22:   'Philosophy' means 'love of wisdom'.

Page 25:   A trireme has three rows of oars.

FURTHER INFORMATION

Books to read

Ancient Greece (Eyewitness) by Anne Pearson (Dorling Kindersley, 2007)

Ancient Greece (Navigators) by Philip Steele (Kingfisher, 2011)

Greek Myths: Stories of Sun, Stone and Sea by Sally Pomme Clayton (Frances Lincoln, 2012)

Treasury of Greek Mythology: Classic Stories of Gods, Goddesses, Heroes & Monsters
   by Donna Jo Napoli (National Geographic, 2011)

Websites

www.ancientgreece.co.uk/

www.bbc.co.uk/schools/primaryhistory/ancient_greeks/

http://greece.mrdonn.org/

http://library.thinkquest.org/CR0210200/ancient_greece/facts.htm

Note to parents and teachers: Every effort has been made by the publishers to ensure that these websites are suitable for children. However, because of the nature of the Internet, it is impossible to guarantee that the contents of these sites will not be altered. We strongly advise that Internet access is supervised by a responsible adult.

Places to visit

Ashmolean Museum, Oxford OX1 2PH

British Museum, London WC1B 3DG

World Museum, Liverpool L3 8EN

INDEX

Numbers in **bold** refer to pictures and captions

THE HISTORY DETECTIVE INVESTIGATES

Contents of all the titles in the series: